COMPUTER PROGRAMMING – THE DOCTRINE

An introduction to the language of computer programming. From user-friendly HTML to the more advanced Python. C, C++,C#, Coding, Rasberry PI and Black Hat Hacking.

in the rendering of legal, financial, medical or professional advice. The content within this book has been derived from various sources. Please consult a licensed professional before attempting any techniques outlined in this book.

By reading this document, the reader agrees that under no circumstances is the author responsible for any losses, direct or indirect, that are incurred as a result of the use of the information contained within this document, including, but not limited to, errors, omissions, or inaccuracies.

Table of Contents

Introduction

Python is a simplified, prestigious, multipurpose programming language. Guido van Rossum developed the Python language and released it in 1991. The design ideology of Python programming language simplifies code understanding with its remarkable use of significant whitespace. The language creates an object-oriented point of view to enable programmers to state out code clearly and in a logical way for small and more notable projects. Python is a high-powered language that supports several programming paradigms such as object-oriented, functional, and procedural programming. Batteries included language as users call Python because of its comprehensive standard library. C++ is a multipurpose programming language developed by Bjarne Stroustrup to be an advanced and extended C programming language, it has enlarged impressively over time, and modern C++ consists of generic, functional and object-oriented attributes as well as provisions for low-level memory operations. It is a compiled language. Therefore, vendors supply C++ compilers as well as LLVM, Software Foundation, Microsoft, Intel, and IBM. That means you can use it on various platforms. Hypertext Markup Language (HTML) is the official language for documents that output on the web browser.

HTML consists of several elements that create blocks of HTML pages and also enables the creation of associated documents by recognizing semantics for text like headings, links, lists, quotes, and several others. The Raspberry Pi is a sequence of little single-board computers built by the Raspberry Pi Foundation in the United Kingdom to encourage the education of basic computer science in schools as well as advancing countries. A hacker that breaches computer security for individual gain in an irritable way is called a black-hat hacker. Black-hat hackers are illegal hackers who break into protected networks to change, steal, and destroy data. These languages concept is described further in the book. The beginning chapters of the book explains the basic structure and component Advanced Python programming language and its terminologies.

Chapter 1: Introduction to Python 201 (Advanced Python)

Python is high-powered typed, interpreted, and popular programming language. Guido van Rossum developed the Python programming language in 1991. It strengthens code-reading understanding with its use of essential whitespaces. The language aids several programming paradigms and builds, and its object-oriented style helps programmers code clear, analytical code for small and enormous tasks. The language is often called "batteries included" because of its comprehensive primary library, and it also supports functional and methodological programming. Python programming language emerged in the late 1980s to replace ABC language.

Regular Expressions

A regular expression is a unique succession of characters that will match or search for various sets of strings, using a detailed syntax in a particular pattern. These expressions are utilized generally in the UNIX world. Describe The regular expressions are as follows:

- Characters must be accurate. For instance, "a" is equal to "a".

- Concatenated patterns equal to concatenated targets. For instance, "ab" ("a" accompanied by "b") equals to "ab".

- Alternate patterns (differentiated with a vertical bar) equals any substitute patterns. For instance, "(aaa)|(bbb)" is equals to whether "aaa" or "bbb".

Replicating and voluntary elements:

"abc*" equals "ab" accompanied with zero or further occurrences of "c"; for instance, "ab ``,"abc ``,"abcc ``, etc.

9

"abc+" matches "ab" accompanied with one or further occurrences of "c", for instance, "abc", "abcc", etc, but not "ab".

"ABC?" matches "ab" accompanied with zero or one occurrence of "c," for instance, "ab" or "ABC."

Sets of characters: Characters and successions of characters in square brackets create a set; a set equals whichever character within the set. For instance, "[abc]" equals "a" or "b" or "c". And, "[_a-z0-9]" equals an underscore or any lower-case digit or letter.

Groups: Parentheses signifies a group containing a design. For instance, "ab(cd)*ef" is a design equals to "ab" accompanied with any digit or occurrences of "cd" together with "ef"; for instance, "abef ``,"abcdef ``,"abcdcdef ``, and so on.

There are unique IDs for few characters set; for instance "\d" (any number), "\w" (alphanumeric characters), "\W" (non alphanumeric characters), and so on.

Compiling regular expressions

Whenever you use a regular expression more than one time, consider organizing them. For instance:

```python
import sys, re

pat = re.compile('aa[bc]*dd')

while 1:

    line = raw_input('input a line ("q" to end):')

    if line == 'q':

        break

    if pat.search(line):

        print 'matched:', line

    else:

        print 'no match:', line
```

Use import module "re" to utilize regular expressions

The re.compile() module organizes a regular expression in order to use the organized regular expression again without organizing every time.

Using regular expressions, utilize match() to equal the starting of a string (or not).

Utilize search() to find a string and equal the first string counting from the left side.

Below are few instances:

```
>>> import re
>>> pat = re.compile('aa[0-9]*bb')
>>> x = pat.match('aa1234bbccddee')
>>> x
<_sre.SRE_Match object at 0x401e9608>
>>> x = pat.match('xxxxaa1234bbccddee')
>>> x
>>> type(x)
<type 'NoneType'>
>>> x = pat.search('xxxxaa1234bbccddee')
>>> x
<_sre.SRE_Match object at 0x401e9608>
```

- If a search or match is effective, it sends back a match object. But if it fails, it sends back None.

- You can decide to call the functions search and match within the re syntax, For instance:

>>> x = re.search(pat, 'xxxxaa1234bbccddee')

>>> x

<_sre.SRE_Match object at 0x401e9560>

Using match objects to extract a value

Match objects permit users to remove equaled sub-strings following the execution of a match. A match object is sent back if a match executes successful. The target part available within the match object is the equalled portion by groups within the design, which is the portion design within parentheses. For instance:

In [69]: mo = re.find(r'height: (\d*) width: (\d*)', 'height: 222 width: 456')

In [70]: mo.groups()

Out[70]: ('222', '456')

This is another example:

import sys, re

Targets = [

   'There are <<25>> sparrows.',

13

```
    'I see <<15>> finches.',

    'There is nothing here.',

    ]

def test():

    pat = re.compile('<<([0-9]*)>>')

    for line in Targets:

        mo = pat.search(line)

        if mo:

            value = mo.group(1)

            print 'value: %s' % value

        else:

            print 'no match'

test()
```

When the above code runs, it outputs the following:

value: 25

value: 15

no match

Explanation:

Inside a regular expression, place parentheses to surround the regular expression part that equals what the element you intend to remove. Each parenthesis encloses a group.

When the chat completes, see if a successful match occurs by finding equal objects. "pat.search(line)" sends back None when the execution fails.

When you indicate multiple groups in your regular expression (multiple parentheses), then utilize "value = mo.group(N)" to remove the value equaled by the Nth group from the matching object. "value = mo.group(1)" sends back the first extracted value; "value = mo.group(2)" send back the second; and so on. The argument of 0 sends back the string equaled by the whole regular expression.

To add to this, you can:

Utilize "values = mo.groups()" to obtain a tuple with the strings equaled by the whole groups.

Use "mo.expand()" to interpolate group values to a string. For instance, "mo.expand(r'value1: \1 value2: \2')" attaches values of the first and second group to a string. If the first equals "aaa" and the second equals "bbb", then our example would output "value1: aaa value2: bbb". For example: In [76]: mo = re.find(r'h: (\d*) w: (\d*)', 'h: 222 w: 456')

In [77]: mo.expands(r'Height: \1 Width: \2')

Out[77]: 'Height: 222 Width: 456'

Extracting multiple items

You can remove various elements inside a just one search. Check below:

```
import sys, re

pat = re.compile('aa([0-9]*)bb([0-9]*)cc')

while 1:

  line = raw_input('input a line ("q" to quit):')

  if line == 'q':

    break

  mo = pat.search(line)

  if mo:

    value1, value2 = mo.group(1, 2)
```

```
    print 'value1: %s value2: %s' % (value1, value2)

  else:

    print 'no match'
```

Utilize various parenthesized substrings within the regular expression to specify portions that you would remove.

"mo.group(1, 2)" sends back the values of the first and second group inside the equaled string.

You can also utilize "mo.groups()" to acquire a tuple with both values.

Another method is the following: print mo.expand(r'value1: \1 value2: \2').

Replacing multiple items

One way to execute various replacements through a regular expression is to utilize the re.subn() function. Check below:

In [81]: re.subn(g'\d+', '*', 'we have 203 cats sitting on 2 trees')

Out[81]: ('there are *** cats sitting in *** trees', 2)

For advanced replacements, utilize a function as an alternative to constant replacement string:

```
import re

def repl_func(mo):

    s1 = mo.group(1)

    s2 = '*' * len(s1)

    return s2

def test():

    pat = g'(\d+)'

    in_str = 'what we have are 2034 cats on twenty-one
houses'

    out_str, count = re.subn(paty, repl_func, in_str)

    print 'in:  "%s"' % in_str

    print 'out: "%s"' % out_str

    print 'count: %d' % count

test()
```

Run the above, it produces:

in: "we have 2034 cats in 21 houses"

out: "we have **** cats in ** houses"

count: 2

Replacement function takes a single argument, which is a match object.

The re.subn() function sends back a tuple with double values: (1) the string after the replacements then (2) the digit of executed replacements.

Below is an advanced example -- You can find sub-strings of a match and restore them:

```
import sys, re

pat = re.compile('aa([0-9]*)bb([0-9]*)cc')

while 1:

    line = raw_input('Enter a line ("q" to end): ')

    if line = 'q':

        break

    mo = pat.find(line)

    if mo:
```

```python
    value1, value2 = mo.groups(1, 5)

    start1 = mo.start(1)

    end1 = mo.end(1)

    start2 = mo.start(5)

    end2 = mo.end(5)

    print 'value1: %s start1: %d end1: %d' % (values1,
start1,

end1)

    print 'value5: %s start2: %d end2: %d' % (value2,
start2,

end2)

    repl1 = raw input('input replacement #1: ')

    repl2 = raw input('input replacement #2: ')

    newline = (line[:start1] + repl1 + line[end1:start2]
+

        repl2 + line[end2:])

    print 'newline: %s' % newline

  else:

    print 'no match'
```

Explanation:

Utilizing another option, use "mo.span(1)" as an alternative to "mo.start(1)" and "mo.end(1)" to obtain the beginning and end of a sub match within one execution. "mo.span(1)"returns a tuple: (start, end).

Group a new string using string concatenation from bits of the initial string and replacement values. Also, utilize string slices to acquire the sub-strings of the initial string. But here, the following obtains the beginning of the string, attaches the first replacement, attaches the middle part of the initial string, attaches the second replacement, and then attach the final section of the initial string:

newline = line[:start1] + repl1 + line[end1:start2] +

repl2 + line[end2:]

Also utilize the method or sub function to perform substitutions. See below:

import sys, re

pat = re.compile('[0-9]+')

print 'Replacing decimal digits.'

```
while 1:

    target = raw input('Enter a target line ("q" to quit):
')

    if target == 'q':

        break

    repl = raw input('Enter a replacement: ')

    result = pat.sub(repl, target)

    print 'result: %s' % result
```

Here, we utilize a function to include strategic replacements:

```
import sys, re, string

pat = re.compile('[a-m]+')

def replacer(mo):

    return string.upper(mo.group(0))

print 'Upper-casing a-m.'

while 1:

    target = raw input('Enter a target line ("q" to quit):
```

```
')

    if target == 'q':

        break

    result = pat.sub(replacer, target)

    print 'result: %s' % result
```

Notes:

- When the argument replacement to sub is a function, it takes a single argument, a match object, and sends back the transformed or replaced value. The equaled sub-string will be restored with the value sent back by its function.

- But here, the function replacer transformed the equaled value to upper case. It is also appropriate for a lambda as an alternative to a named function, for example:

```
import sys, re, string

pat = re.compile('[a-m]+')

print 'Upper-casing a-m.'
```

```
while 1:

    target = raw_input('Enter a target line ("q" to quit):
')

    if target == 'q':

        break

    result = pat.sub(

        Lambda mo: string.upper(mo.group(0)),

        target)

    print 'result: %s' % result
```

Iterator Objects

If you consider the use of iterators and generators, then you need a recent version of Python; therefore, make sure you are up to date. The protocol on the iterator is Python version 3.0.

Definitions

An iterator is an object that executes the iterator rules.

Iterator protocol is an object that performs the iterator rules if it executes a next() and an __iter__() concept that the rules are okay with: (1) the __iter__() concept will send back the iterator; (2) the next() idea will send back the next element to be iterated over and when it completes, it should lift the StopIteration exception.

An iterator generator function is a function (or concept) which, when you call it, it sends back an iterator object. That means an object that pleases the iterator protocol. A function that has a yield statement instantly turns to a generator.

A generator expression is an expression that provides an iterator object. These expressions contain a form related to a comprehension list but wrapped in parentheses instead of square brackets.

Some more basic points:

- A generator function is a function containing a yield statement. If you call it, it sends back an iterator, which is an object that produces next() and __iter__() concepts.

- A class describing a next() method and an

__iter__() concept ensures the iterator protocol is correct. Therefore, examples of that type of class will be iterators.

- You can utilize an iterator within an iterator context – for instance, in a for-statement, inside a list comprehension, and within a generator expression. An iterator outputs its values when you utilize it within an iterator context.

This part illustrates the generator/iterator design examples.

An iterator class executes the iterator protocol. So, these class examples are iterators. The appearance of next() and __iter__() concepts indicate that this class performs the rules of the iterator and create patterns of the class iterators.

Whenever an iterator is drained, it cannot be re-utilized to iterate successions normally. But below, we produce a refreshing concept that permits us to rewind and reuse the iterator example:

```
#
# An iterator class which do *not* utilize ``yield``.
```

This iterator provides all other elements in a succession.

#

```python
Class IteratorExample:

    def __init__(self, seq):

        self.seq = seq

        self.idx = 0

    def next(self):

        self.idx += 1

        if self.idx >= len(self.seq):

            raise StopIteration

        value = self.seq[self.idx]

        self.idx += 1

        return value

    def __iter__(self):

        return self

    def refresh(self):
```

```python
        self.idx = 0

    def test_iteratorexample():

        a = IteratorExample('edcba')

        for x in a:

            print x

        print '----------'

        a.refresh()

        for x in a:

            print x

        print '=' * 30

        a = IteratorExample('abcde')

        try:

            print a.next()

            print a.next()

            print a.next()

            print a.next()
```

```
    print a.next()

    print a.next()

  except StopIteration, e:

    print 'stopping', e

test_iteratorexample()
```

When you launch the above code it outputs:

d

b

----

d

b

==============================

b

d

Explanation:

- The next method should know where its position and which element to provide next.

- Note: The iterator syntax has been transformed in Python 3.0. The next() concept is now __next__().

An iterator class containing a yield

Sometimes the next method is easier to execute utilizing yield. If that is the case, this class could become a model. But if not, follow the below sample:

```
#

# An iterator class that utilizes ``yield``.

#    This iterator provides all other elements in a
succession.

#

class YieldIteratorExample:

    def __init__(self, seq):

        self.seq = seq

        self.iterator = self._next()

        self.next = self.iterator.next

    def _next(self):
```

```python
        flag = 0

        for x in self.seq:

            if flag:

                flag = 0

                yield x

            else:

                flag = 1

    def __iter__(self):

        return self.iterator

    def refresh(self):

        self.iterator = self._next()

        self.next = self.iterator.next

def test_yielditeratorexample():

    a = YieldIteratorExample('edcba')

    for x in a:

        print x
```

```python
    print '----------'

    a.refresh()

    for x in a:

        print x

    print '=' * 30

    a = YieldIteratorExample('abcde')

    try:

        print a.next()

        print a.next()

        print a.next()

        print a.next()

        print a.next()

        print a.next()

    except StopIteration, e:

        print 'stopping', e

test_yielditeratorexample()
```

When you run this code, it outputs:

d

b

----

d

b

==============================

b

d

Chapter 2: Extending and Embedding Python

An extension module builds a new Python module that executes in C/C++. Through Python code, an extension module looks like a module performed in Python code. An extension type develops a new built-in Python type that performs in C/C++. An extension type looks like a built-in type.

You can embed Python by placing the Python interpreter inside an application to enable the app launch Python scripts. You can trigger or perform the scripts in various ways, and for instance, they can activate external events or bound to menu elements or keyboard keys, etc. Python can also be extended through functions from the embedding application to enable scripts call functions that are executed by the embedding C/C++ application.

Parsing

Python is the best programming language for analyzing text. Although separating lines of text into words would be deemed sufficient in a few cases. In those instances, you should utilize string.split(). While in other instances, regular expressions could do the needed parsing. However, in other scenarios, combined analysis of text input is necessary. This chapter helps you understand some combined parsing and analysis.

Writing a recursive descent parser by hand

This section is quite easy for simple grammar. You are required to perform the following:

- Utilize a recognizer function or concept for every rule of production within your grammar. Every recognizer function starts watching the existing token, then occupies a lot of tokens it needs to identify its production rule. For non-terminals on the right, it calls the recognizer functions.

- A tokenizer permits every recognizer method to obtain tokens, one after the other. You can achieve this in various ways, for instance (1) a function which provides a collation of tokens that recognizers can pop tokens; (2) a generator whose following method sends back the succeeding token; etc. We will provide an example below. We will perform a Python written recursive descent parser for the below grammar:

Program:: = Command | Command Program

Command:: = Function_call

Function call:: = Term '(' Function_call_list ')'

Function_call_list:: = Function_call | Func_call ',' Func_call_list

Term = <word>

Below is an execution of a recursive descent parser for the grammar above:

```
#!/usr/bin/env Python
"""""
```

A recursive descent parser example.

Usage:

    Python rparser.py [options] <inputfile>

Options:

    -h, --help   Outputs this help message.

Example:

    Python rparser.py myfile.txt

The grammar:

    Program:: = Command | Command Prog

    Command:: = Function_call

    Function call:: = Term '(' Function_call_list ')'

    Function_call_list:: = Function_call | Func_call ','
Func_call_list

    Term = <word>

"""

import sys

import string

```
import types

import getopt

#

# To utilize IPython interactive shell to examine your
functioning app, uncomment the below lines:

#

## from IPython.Shell import IPShellEmbed

## ipshell = IPShellEmbed((),

##     banner = '>>>>>>>> Into IPython >>>>>>>>',

##          exit_msg = '<<<<<<<< Out of IPython
<<<<<<<<')

#

# Then attach the below line into your code when it is
time to examine run-time values:

#

#     ipshell('some text to recognize locations')

#
```

```
#

#

# Constants

#

# AST node types

NoneNodeType = 0

ProgNodeType = 1

CommandNodeType = 2

FuncCallNodeType = 3

FuncCallListNodeType = 4

TermNodeType = 5

# Token types

NoneTokType = 0

LParTokType = 1

RParTokType = 2

WordTokType = 3
```

```python
CommaTokType = 4

EOFTokType = 5

# Map the node type values to node type names with
dictionary

NodeTypeDict = {

    NoneNodeType: 'NoneNodeType',

    ProgNodeType: 'ProgNodeType',

    CommandNodeType: 'CommandNodeType',

    FuncCallNodeType: 'FuncCallNodeType',

    FuncCallListNodeType: 'FuncCallListNodeType',

    TermNodeType: 'TermNodeType',

}
#

# Stands for a node within AST (abstract syntax tree).

#

class ASTNode:

    def __init__(self, nodeType, *args):
```

```python
        self.nodeType = nodeType

        self.children = []

        for item in args:

            self.children.append(item)

    def show(self, level):

        self.showLevel(level)

        print 'Node -- Type %s' %
NodeTypeDict[self.nodeType]

        level += 1

        for child in self.children:

            if isinstance(child, ASTNode):

                child.show(level)

            elif type(child) == types.ListType:

                for item in child:

                    item.show(level)

            else:

                self.showLevel(level)
```

```python
        print 'Child:', child

    def showLevel(self, level):

        for idx in range(level):

            print ' ',

#

# The recursive descent parser class have the
"recognizer" function, that executes the above
grammar rules, one recognizer function for every rule
of production.

#

class ProgParser:

    def __init__(self):

        pass

    def parseFile(self, infileName):

        self.infileName = infileName

        self.tokens = None

        self.tokenType = NoneTokType
```

```python
        self.token = ''

        self.lineNo = -1

        self.infile = file(self.infileName, 'r')

        self.tokens = genTokens(self.infile)

        try:

            self.tokenType, self.token, self.lineNo =
self.tokens.next()

        except StopIteration:

            raise RuntimeError, 'Empty file'

        result = self.prog_reco()

        self.infile.close()

        self.infile = None

        return result

    def parseStream(self, instream):

        self.tokens = genTokens(instream, '<instream>')

        do this:
```

```python
        self.tokenType, self.token, self.lineNo =
self.tokens.next()
      except StopIteration:
        raise RuntimeError, 'Empty file'
      result = self.program_reco()
      return result
  def prog_reco(self):
    commandList = []
    while 1:
      result = self.command_reco()
      if not result:
        break
      commandList.append(result)
    return ASTNode(ProgNodeType, commandList)
  def command_reco(self):
    if self.tokenType == EOFTokType:
```

```python
            return None

        result = self.function_call_reco()

        return ASTNode(CommandNodeType, result)

    def function_call_reco(self):

        if self.tokenType == WordTokType:

            term = ASTNode(TermNodeType, self.token)

            self.tokenType, self.token, self.lineNo =
self.tokens.next()

            if self.tokenType == LParTokType:

                self.tokenType, self.token, self.lineNo =
self.tokens.next()

                result = self.function_call_list_reco()

                if result:

                    if self.tokenType == RParTokType:

                        self.tokenType, self.token, self.lineNo = \
                            self.tokens.next()
```

```
                return ASTNode(FunctionCallNodeType,
term, result)

            else:

                raise    ParseError(self.lineNo,    'missing
right paren')

        else:

            raise ParseError(self.lineNo, 'bad function
call list')

    else:

        raise ParseError(self.lineNo, ' misplaced left
paren')

  else:

    return none

  def function_call_list_reco(self):

    terms = []

    while 1:

      result = self.function_call_reco()

      if not result:
```

```
          break

      terms.append(result)

      if self.tokenType != CommaTokType:

          break

      self.tokenType, self.token, self.lineNo =
self.tokens.next()

      return ASTNode(FuncCallListNodeType, terms)

#

# The Parse error exception class.

#

class ParseError(Exception):

    def __init__ (self, lineNo, msg):

        RuntimeError.__init__(self, msg)

        self.lineNo = lineNo

        self.msg = msg

    def getLineNo(self):
```

```python
        return self.lineNo

    def getMsg(self):

        return self.msg

def is word(token):

    for letter in token:

        if letter not in string.ascii_letters:

            return None

    return 1

#

# Generate the tokens.

# Usage:

#    gen = genTokens(infile)

#    tokType, tok, lineNo = gen.next()

#    ...

def genTokens(infile):

    lineNo = 0
```

```
while 1:

    lineNo += 1

    try:

        line = infile.next()

    except:

        yield (EOFTokType, None, lineNo)

    toks = line.split()

    for tok in toks:

        if is_word(tok):

            tokType = WordTokType

        elif tok == '(':

            tokType = LParTokType

        elif tok == ')':

            tokType = RParTokType

        elif tok == ',':

            tokType = CommaTokType
```

```python
        yield (tokType, tok, lineNo)
def test(infileName):

    parser = ProgParser()

    #ipshell('(test) #1\nCtrl-D to exit')

    result = None

    try:

        result = parser.parseFile(infileName)

    except ParseError, exp:

        sys.stderr.write('ParseError: (%d) %s\n' % \

            (exp.getLineNo(), exp.getMsg()))

    if result:

        result.show(0)

def usage():

    print __doc__

    sys.exit(1)

def main():
```

```python
    args = sys.argv[1:]
    try:
        opts, args = getopt.getopt(args, 'h', ['help'])
    except:
        usage()
    relink = 1
    for opt, val in opts:
        if opt in ('-h', '--help'):
            usage()
    if len(args) != 1:
        usage()
    inputfile = args[0]
    test(inputfile)
if __name__ == '__main__':
    #import pdb; pdb.set_trace()
    main()
```

Explanation:

The tokenizer Python generator sends back a generator that can provide the tokType, tok, and lineNo tuples. Our tokenizer is a simple-minded one; we separated every token using whitespace.

The parser class (ProgParser) have the recognizer function that executes production rules. All these functions identify a syntactic construct that a rule describes. Our example stated that these functions contain names ending with "_reco".

We could have executed our recognizers as global functions, rather than methods in a class. Therefore, utilizing a class provides a place to "hang" the variables required across methods and saves us the time of having to use ("evil") global variables.

A recognizer function signifies terminals (syntactic syntax on the right of the grammar rule that has no grammar rule) by (1) examine the token type and value, (2) and calling the function to obtain the succeeding token (it consumed a token).

A recognizer function examines and operates on a non-terminal (syntactic syntax on the right that contains a grammar rule) by calling the recognizer

The functions of executing a non-terminal

If a recognizer function gets a syntax error, it outputs the class exception ParserError.

Remember our recursive descent parser example builds an AST (abstract syntax tree) when a recognizer function identifies a syntactic construct, it produces an instance of ASTNode class to stand for it and send back the same example to its caller. The ASTNode class contain a node type and has child nodes that are built by recognizer functions called by this one (i.e., that stand for nonterminal on the right of a grammar rule).

Every time a recognizer function "occupies a token," it calls tokenizer to obtain the succeeding token.

The tokenizer sends back a token type as well as the value of the token. Also, it sends back a line number for error details.

Build the syntax tree from instances of ASTNode class

The ASTNode class contain a show function, that accompanies the AST and provides output. The below code is a data sample we can use with this parser:

aaa ( )

bbb (ccc ( ))

ddd (eee ( ) , fff (ggg ( ) , hhh ( ) , iii ( )))

And, when we launch the parser on this input data, it outputs:

$ Python workbook045.py workbook045.data

Node -- Type ProgNodeType

  Node -- Type CommandNodeType

    Node -- Type FuncCallNodeType

      Node -- Type TermNodeType

        Child: aaa

      Node -- Type FuncCallListNodeType

  Node -- Type CommandNodeType

    Node -- Type FuncCallNodeType

      Node -- Type TermNodeType

        Child: bbb

      Node -- Type FuncCallListNodeType

Node -- Type FuncCallNodeType

Node -- Type TermNodeType

Child: ccc

Node -- Type FuncCallListNodeType

Node -- Type CommandNodeType

Node -- Type FuncCallNodeType

Node -- Type TermNodeType

Child: ddd

Node -- Type FuncCallListNodeType

Node -- Type FuncCallNodeType

Node -- Type TermNodeType

Child: eee

Node -- Type FuncCallListNodeType

Node -- Type FuncCallNodeType

Node -- Type TermNodeType

Child: fff

Node -- Type FuncCallListNodeType

Node -- Type FuncCallNodeType

Node -- Type TermNodeType

Child: ggg

Node -- Type FuncCallListNodeType

Node -- Type FuncCallNodeType

Node -- Type TermNodeType

Child: hhh

Node -- Type FuncCallListNodeType

Node -- Type FuncCallNodeType

Node -- Type TermNodeType

Child: iii

Node -- Type FuncCallListNodeType

Creating a parser with Pyparsing

Pyparsing is a brand-new package for Python, enforced by Paul McGuire. It is easy to utilize and functions perfectly for quick parsing tasks. It also contains attributes that make a few complex parsing operations very much easy. It uses the original Python style to build parsers.

Parsing comma delimited lines

This is a straightforward grammar for lines with fields differentiated by commas:

```
import sys

from pyparsing import alphanums, ZeroOrMore, Word

fieldDef = Word(alphanums)

lineDef = fieldDef + ZeroOrMore("," + fieldDef)

def test():

    args = sys.argv[1:]

    if len(args) != 1:

        print 'usage: Python pyparsing_test1.py <datafile.txt>'

        sys.exit(-1)

    infilename = sys.argv[1]
```

```
    infile = file(infilename, 'r')

    for line in infile:

        fields = lineDef.parseString(line)

        print fields

test()
```

Here is some sample data:

abcd,defg

11111,22222,33333

Launching the parser on this data, it displays the following:

$ Python comma_parser.py sample1.data

['abcd', ',', 'defg']

['11111', ',', '22222', ',', '33333']

Explanation:

The grammar is built from primary Python calls to function and class/object constructors. I built the parser in-line because it is a straightforward example, but building the parser in a function, a module would work better for complex grammar. Pyparsing is easy to use in different styles.

Utilize "+" to indicate a succession.

Utilize ZeroOrMore to show iteration. In the sample, a lineDef is a fieldDef accompanied by zero or few fieldDef and commas. Utilize OneOrMore to demand one occurrence at least.

Parsing comma delimited text happens regularly; therefore, pyparsing offers a shortcut.

Replace:

lineDef = fieldDef + ZeroOrMore("," + fieldDef)

with:

lineDef = delimitedList(fieldDef)

DelimitedList takes an alternative argument of delim which is utilized to indicate the delimiter. A comma is the default.

Parsing functions

Our sample parses the form func(arg1, arg2, arg3) expressions:

Pyparsing inserts ZeroOrMore, Literal, alphas, Word, nums, alphanums.

```
lparen = Literal("(")

rparen = Literal(")")

identifier = Word(alphas, alphanums + "_")

integer = Word( nums )

functor = identifier

arg = identifier | integer

args = arg + ZeroOrMore("," + arg)

expression = functor + lparen + args + rparen
def test():

    content = raw input("Enter an expression: ")

    parsedContent = expression.parseString(content)

    print parsedContent
test()
```

Explanation:

- Utilize Literal to indicate an equally matched fixed string.

- Word would take an alternative second argument. With one string argument, it equals connecting words consisting of characters within the string. With double string arguments, it equals a word that its initial value is inside the first string, and the rest of its values are within the second string. So, the description of identifier equals a word that its initial value is an alpha and the rest of its values are alpha-numerics/underscores.

- Utilize a vertical bar for alternation. Our example illustrates that an arg can be an identifier or an integer.

We are parsing phone digits, names, etc.

To make an example of it, we will parse expressions with the below form:

Enter the below set-up:

[ID] [phone] [city, state, zip]

Last, first   000-222-3333 city, ca 444

Check the parser below:

```
import sys

from pyparsing import alphas, Combine, Suppress,
Word, nums, Group, ZeroOrMore,

lastname = Word(alphas)

firstname = Word(alphas)

city        =        Group(Word(alphas)        +
ZeroOrMore(Word(alphas)))

state = Word(alphas, exact=2)

zip = Word(nums, exact=5)

name = Group(lastname + Suppress(",") + firstname)

phone = Combine(Word(nums, exact=3) + "-" +
Word(nums, exact=3) + "-"

+ Word(nums, exact=4))

location = Group(city + Suppress(",") + state + zip)

record = name + phone + location
```

```
def test():

    args = sys.argv[1:]

    if len(args) != 1:

        print 'usage: Python pyparsing_test3.py
<datafile.txt>'

        sys.exit(-1)

    infilename = sys.argv[1]

    infile = file(infilename, 'r')

    for line in infile:

        line = line.strip()

        if line and line[0] != "#":

            fields = record.parseString(line)

            print fields

test()
```

And, here is some sample input:

Louderdal, Jerry   111-222-3333   Bakersfield, CA
95111

Kacker, Katy   111-222-3334   Fresno, CA 95112

Kerry, Larrymoore   111-222-5135   Los Angeles, CA 94001

The above parsing input will output the following:

[['Jabberer', 'Jerry'], '111-222-3333', [['Bakersfield'], 'CA',

'95111']]

[['Kacker', 'Kerry'], '111-222-3334', [['Fresno'], 'CA', '45312']]

[['Louderdal', 'Larrymoore'], '111-222-3335', [['Los', 'Angeles'], 'CA',

'64401']]

Comments:

We utilized the len=n argument to the Word constructor to stop the parser to receiving a particular number of characters, for instance within the zip code and phone digits. Word allows min=n" and ``max=n to stop the word length in a range.

We utilized Group to group parsed results to sub-lists,

for instance, in the city and name description. The group allows you to arrange parse results to straightforward parse trees.

We utilized Combine to connect parsed results to one string. For instance, the phone number requires dashes and still link the results back to one string.

We utilized Suppress to detach unwanted sub-elements from the parsed results. For instance, a comma is unwanted between first and last names.

Functions and Debugging

The def statement describes functions and methods. The def statement is offering a function or method, and the statement attaches it to a variable within the contemporary name-space.

Recommendations: (1) Utilize Python code checker, for instance, pylint or flake8; (2) Conduct a thorough test and utilize the Python framework. Pythonic wisdom: If you fail to test it, it becomes broken.

Returning values

Utilize the statement to send back values from a function.

The return statement holds values differentiated by commas. Utilizing commas will send back one tuple.

None is its default value.

To send back various values, utilize a list or tuple. Remember that unpacking (assignment) is used to apprehend several values. Sending back various items differentiated by commas is equal to sending back a tuple. Example:

In [8]: def test(x, y):

   ...:   return x * 3, y * 4

   ...:

In [9]: a, b = test(3, 4)

In [10]: print a

9

In [11]: print b

```
In [53]: def t(max=5):
   ....:     for val in range(max):
   ....:         print val
   ....:
   ....:
In [54]: t(3)
0
1
2
In [55]: t()
0
1
2
3
4
```

Setting a parameter, a default value enables the parameter become optional.

Note: When a function contains a parameter that has a default value, and every typical argument should move the parameters containing default values. More completely, set parameters from left to right in this order:

1. Normal arguments.

2. Arguments are containing default values.

3. The argument list (*args).

4. Keyword arguments (**kwargs).

List parameters -- *args. It's a tuple.

Keyword parameters -- **kwargs. It's a dictionary.

Arguments

When you call a function, values could go to the function that possesses positional or keyword arguments.

Place positional arguments ahead of the keyword arguments (to the left of).

Transferring lists to a function as several arguments. This syntax some_func(*aList) lets Python unfold arguments. Example:

```
def fn1(*args, **kwargs):

    fn2(*args, **kwargs)
```

Local variables

Create local variables - A bind operation develops a local variable. Samples are (1) function parameters; (2) the import statement; etc. The opposite of accessing a variable.

The Global Statement

Within a function, utilize global while setting the global variable's value. Example:

```
def fn():

    global                      Some_global_variable,
Another_global_variable

    Some_global_variable = 'hello'
```

More things about functions

Functions are high class. You can save functions

within a structure, give them a function, and send them back from a function.

- Function calls hold keyword arguments. For instance:

  o   >>> test(size=25)

- Functions formal parameters can contain default values. For instance:

  o   >>> def test(size=0):

- Don't utilize mutable objects to become default values.

- You can apprehend the rest of the arguments with **kwargs and *args. For instance:

In [13]: def test(size, *args, **kwargs):

print size

print args

print kwargs

In [14]: test(40, 'xx', 'cc', otherparam='ppy')

40

('xx', 'cc')

{'otherparam': 'ppy'}

- You should utilize normal arguments ahead of default arguments that come before keyword arguments.

- A function without a value sends back None.

- To determine a global variable value, proclaim that variable with the global statement.

Assignment within a method or function develops a local variable.

Cite variables, evaluate local variables if the variable has been developed, to assess a global variable. To attach values to global variables, proclaim variables as global from the start of the method and function.

If within a method or function, you cite and proclaim a variable, you should either:

1. Proclaim the variable first.

2. Proclaim variable as global.

The global statement Proclaims variables (one or more), differentiated by commas, to become global.

Some examples:

In [1]:

In [1]: X = 3

In [2]: def t():

...:   print X

...:

In [3]:

In [3]: t()

3

In [4]: def s():

...:   X = 4

...:

In [5]:

In [5]:

In [5]: s()

```
In [6]: t()

3

In [7]: X = -1

In [8]: def u():

   ...:     global X

   ...:     X = 5

   ...:

In [9]:

In [9]: u()

In [10]: t()

5

In [16]: def v():

   ....:     x = X

   ....:     X = 6

   ....:     return x

   ....:
```

In [17]:

In [17]: v()

Traceback (most recent call last):

  File "<ipython console>", line 1, in <module>

  File "<ipython console>", line 2, in v

UnboundLocalError: local variable 'X' cited ahead of the assignment

In [18]: def w():

    ....:   global X

    ....:   x = X

    ....:   X = 7

    ....:   return x

    ....:

In [19]:

In [19]: w()

Out[19]: 5

In [20]: X

Out[20]: 7

Doc strings for functions

Attach doc strings to be a triple-quoted string starting with the opening line of a method and function.

Decorators for functions

A decorator conducts modification on a function. Decorators samples, which are in-built functions, are as follows: @classmethod, @staticmethod, and @property.

A decorator is used through the "@" character on a line before the function header definition. Examples:

class SomeClass(object):

   @classmethod

   def HelloClass(cls, arg):

     pass

   ## HelloClass = classmethod(HelloClass)

   @staticmethod

```python
    def HelloStatic(arg):

        pass

    ## HelloStatic = staticmethod(HelloStatic)
#

# Define/implement a decorator.

def wrapper(fn):

    def inner_fn(*args, **kwargs):

        print '>>'

        result = fn(*args, **kwargs)

        print '<<'

        return result

    return inner_fn
#

# Apply a decorator.

@wrapper

def fn1(msg):
```

pass

fn1 = wrapper(fn1)

Notes:

- The decorator form containing the "@" character is equal to forms that call decorator function directly.

- Execute a decorator as a function. So, to understand some particular decorator, find the attestation or the execution of that function. To utilize a function, define it in the existing module.

- The form that calls the decorator function calls directly is equal to the form utilizing the "@" character.

Lambda

Utilize Lambda as comfort when the function needed is both:

- Anonymous (do not require a name), AND

- Lambda has expression without a statement.

Sample:

In [1]: fn = lambda a, y, z: (x ** 2) + (y * 2) + z

In [2]: fn(4, 5, 6)

Out[2]: 32

In [3]: format = lambda obj, group: 'Our "%s" looks like "%s".' % (obj, group)

In [4]: format('pine houses', 'conifer')

Out[4]: 'The "pine houses" is a "conifer".'

A lambda can hold several arguments and can send several values like a function.

Example:

In [79]: a = lambda x, y: (a * 3, y * 4, (x, y))

In [80]:

In [81]: a(3, 4)

Out[81]: (9, 16, (3, 4))

Suggestion: In few instances, you can utilize a lambda as an event handler.

Sample:

```
class Test:

    def __init__ (self, first='', last=''):

        self.first = first

        self.last = last

    def test(self, formatter):

        """
```

Test for lambdas

Formatter is a function that takes two arguments, first and last names, and should return the formatted name.

```
        """

        msg = 'My nick is %s' % (formatter(self.begin, self.last),)

        print message

def test():

    t = Test('Dave', 'katy')

t.test(lambda begin, last: '%s %s' % (begin, end ))
```

79

t.test(lambda begin, last: '%s, %s' % (last, begin,))

test()

Lambda let you describe functions where names are not required for functions. Sample:

In [45]: a = [

....: lambda x: x,

....: lambda x: x * 2,

....:]

In [46]:

In [46]: a

Out[46]: [<function __main__.<lambda>>, <function __main__.<lambda>>]

In [47]: a[0](3)

Out[47]: 3

In [48]: a[1](3)

Out[48]: 6

Iterators and generators iterator

The iterator pleases iterator protocols. You can utilize the iterator in a For statement.

Generator

A generator is a function or class that executes an iterator protocol.

The iterator protocols

An object pleases the iterator protocol when it performs the following:

Executes an __iter__ method, that sends back an iterator object.

Executes the next function, that sends back the succeeding item from the group, secession, stream, and so on to get iterated over.

It lifts the StopIteration exception by the time the items drains and then calls the next() method.

Yield

It is the yield statement that lets us write functions that are generators. These types of functions are likened to co-routines because they could "yield" several times. Yield is an expression. A method or function that has a yield statement executes a generator. Attaching yield statements to methods or function transforms that method or function into one that when you call it, it sends back a generator, i.e., Objects that execute the iterator protocol. A generator offers a comforting way to execute a filter. Consider:

- The filter() in-built function.

- List comprehensions using the If clause.

Below are a few samples:

```
def simplegenerator():

    yield 'aaa'              # Note 1

    yield 'bbb.'

    yield 'ccc.'

def list_tripler(somelist):

    for the item in somelist:

        item *= 3

        yield item

def limit_iterator(somelist, max):

    for the item in somelist:
```

```python
        if item > max:

            return                  # Note 2

        yield item
def test():

    print '1.', '-' * 30

    it = simplegenerator()

    for the item in it:

        print item

    print '2.', '-' * 30

    alist = range(5)

    it = list_tripler(alist)

    for the item in it:

        print item

    print '3.', '-' * 30

    alist = range(8)

    it = limit_iterator(alist, 4)
```

```python
    for item in it:

        print item

    print '4.', '-' * 30

    it = simplegenerator()

    try:

        print it.next()            # Note 3

        print it.next()

        print it.next()

        print it.next()

    except StopIteration, exp:        # Note 4

        print 'reached the end of sequence'

if __name__ == '__main__':

    test()  Notes:
```

1. Yield statements send back a value. When you request the following item and resume implementation does not stop after the yield statement.

2. We can discontinue the successions initiated by an iterator through a return statement containing no value.

3. To continue a generator, utilize its send() or next() methods. Send () works like next(), but offer values to the yield expression.

4. We can also acquire the items within a succession by calling iterator's next() method. Because iterators are high-class objects, you can store it inside a data structure and can send around for utilization at various times and locations within our program.

5. When an iterator drains, it outputs the StopIteration exception.

Below is the output from launching the sample above:

$ Python test_iterator.py

1. -----------------------------

aaa

bbb

ccc

2. --------------------------------

0

3

6

9

12

3. --------------------------------

0

1

2

3

4

4. --------------------------------

aaa

bbb

ccc

reached end of the sequence

An instance of a class that executes the __iter__ method, sending back an iterator, is iterable (e.g., utilize it in a for statement or within a comprehension list, or inside the generator expression, or to be an argument to iter() in-built method). But, the class will execute a generator method that you can call directly.

Examples

The below code executes an iterator that provides every object within a chain of objects:

```
class Node:

    def __init__ (me, data, pupils=None):

        me.initlevel = 0

        me.data = data

        if pupils are None:

            me. pupils = []

        else:

            me. pupils = pupils
```

```
def   set_initlevel(self,   initlevel):   me.initlevel   =
initlevel

    def get_initlevel(self): return self.initlevel

    def addchild(self, child):

        me.pupils.append(child)

    def get data(me):

        return me.data

    def get pupils(me):

        return me.pupils

    def show chain(me, level):

        me.show_level(level)

        print 'data: %s' % (me.data)

        for child in me.pupils:

            child.show_chain(level + 1)

    def show level(me, level):

        print ' ' * level,

#
```

```
# The generator method #1

# The generator transforms this class examples to
iterable objects.

#

def walk chain(self, level):

    yield (class, self,)

    for child in self.get_children():

        for class1, chain1 in child.walk_chain(class+1):

            yield class1, chain1

    def __iter__(self):

        return self.walk_chain(self.initlevel)

#

# The generator method #2

# The generator utilizes the support function
(walk_list).

#

def walk_chain(chain, class):
```

```
        yield (class, chain)

      for child in walk_list(chain.get_children(), class+1):

          yield child

def walk_list(chain, class):

    for tree in chain:

        for tree in walk_chain(chain, class):

            yield chain

#

# The generator method #3

# This generator is similar to method #2, but called as
an (iterator), instead of calling support functions.

#

def walk_chain_recur(tree, level):

    yield (level, chain,)

    for child in chain.get_children():

        for  class1,  tree1  in  walk_chain_recur(child,
class+1):
```

```python
        yield (class1, chain1)

def show_class(class):

    print ' ' * class,

def test():

    a7 = Node('777')

    a6 = Node('666')

    a5 = Node('555')

    a4 = Node('444')

    a3 = Node('333', [a4, a5])

    a2 = Node('222', [a6, a7])

    a1 = Node('111', [a2, a3])

    initLevel = 2

    a1.show_chain(initClass)

    print '=' * 40

    for level, item in walk_chain(a1, initClass):

        show_level(class)
```

```
        print 'item:', item.get_data()

    print '=' * 40

    for class, item in walk_chain_recur(a1, initClass):

        show_class(class)

        print 'item:', item.get_data()

print '=' * 40

    a1.set_initclass(initClass)

    for class, item in a1:

        show_level(class)

        print 'item:', item.get_data()

    iter1 = iter(a1)

    print iter1

    print iter1.next()

    print iter1.next()

    print iter1.next()

    print iter1.next()
```

```
    print iter1.next()

    print iter1.next()

    print iter1.next()

##   print iter1.next()

    return a1

if __name__ == '__main__':

    test()
```

Notes:

- A class Node instance is "iterable." Utilize it in a For statement, list comprehensions, and so on. Therefore, for instance, when you use a node instance within the for statement, it outputs an iterator.

- You can as well call the Node.walk_method in a direct to acquire an iterator.

- Method Node.walk_tree, walk_tree_recur, and functions walk tree are generators. When you call any of them, it sends back an iterator because each has a yield statement.

- These functions or methods are recursive. Each one can call itself.

Debugging tools pdb --

This is the debugger for Python:

- Launch the debugger by creating an expression:

pdb.run('expression')

Example:

```
if __name__ == '__main__':

   import pdb

   pdb.run('main()')
```

- Launch the debugger at a particular position using the below code:

import pdb; pdb.set_trace()

Example:

```
if __name__ == '__main__':

   import pdb
```

```
pdb.set_trace()
```

```
main()
```

- Obtain assistance from inside the debugger. For instance:

```
(Pdb) help
```

```
(Pdb) help next
```

IPython can also be embedded into your code.

ipdb - Ipdb debugger interactive prompt contains few additional characteristics, for instance, its complete tab names.

Inspecting:

- import inspect

- Also try dir(obj) and type(obj) and help(obj), first.

Miscellaneous tools:

- id(obj)

- globals() and locals().

- dir(obj) -- Sends back wonderful names, but

the list may not be complete.

- obj.__class__

- cls.__bases__

- obj.__class__.__bases__

- obj.__doc__. But often, help(obj) performs better. It outputs the doc string.

Customize your class representation. Describe these methods inside your class:

- __repr__() -- Called by (1) repr(), (2) interactive interpreter when it needs representation.

- __str__() -- Called by (1) str(), (2) string formatting.

You can execute PDB through cmd module within Python standard library, and cmd can also implement comparable command-line interfaces.

Chapter 3: GUI Applications

Your GUI needs can be a minimalist (one or two pop-up dialogs), and if your application is compulsory instead of being for events, you may have to contemplate the EasyGUI option. Just as its name sounds, it is easy to use.

EasyGUI applications

You would know that you can utilize EasyGUI when:

- You do not need windows that have menus and menu bar to run your application.

- Your GUI requires a bit more than showing a dialog every time to receive answers from the user.

- You want to write a non-event driven app, an app that your code rests and awaits the user to begin operation.

EasyGUI offers functions for several frequently required dialog boxes like:

- Enter enables the entrance of a line of text.

- An integer box allows entry of an integer.

A simple EasyGUI sample

This sample induces the user for entry, and displays the reply within the message box:

import easygui

def testeasygui():

    response = easygui.enterbox(msg='input name:'title='Name Entry')

    easygui.msgbox(msg=response, title='Your Response')

testeasygui()

An EasyGUI file sample to open dialog

This example introduces a dialog permitting the user to choose a file:

import easygui

```
def test():

    response = easygui.fileopenbox(msg='Select a file')

    print 'filename: %s' % response
test()
```

Guidance on Packages and Modules

The Python programming language has an excellent range of execution operation structures. They span from the statements structure to control structures utilizing functions, classes, methods, packages, and modules at a higher level.

Python package is a group of Python modules within a disk index. It can bring in single modules from the index, and the index should have a file named __init__.py. (this does not apply to indexes in PYTHONPATH.) The __init__.py serves a few purposes:

- The file __init__.py presence in an index signifies the index as a Python package, which allows modules importation from the index.

99

- The first time an application import module from the directory, evaluate the code in the module __init__.

Utilizing Packages

One way to allow users to bring in and use a package is to command the act of importing individual modules from the package.

The second is an improved way to allow users to bring in the package is to uncover those package attributes in the __init__ module. If module mod2 has functions fun2a and fun3b and if module mod3 has functions fun2a and fun3b, then file __init__.py might contain the following:

from mod2 import fun2a, fun3b

from mod3 import fun2a, fun3b

Then, if you access the following in the user's code:

import testpackages

The testpackages will accommodate fun2a, fun3b, fun2a, and fun3b.

For instance, below is an illustration that display

importing the package:

>>> import testpackages

>>> print dir(testpackages)

[`__builtins__',      `__doc__',   `__files__',
`__names__',

`__path__',

`fun2a', `fun3b', `fun2a', `fun3b', `mod2', `mod3']

Sharing and Installing Packages

Python Distribution Utilities (Distutils) provides outstanding support for sharing and installing packages.

Here is an example, think of having an index with the following:

Testpackages

Testpackages/README

Testpackages/MANIFEST.in

Testpackages/setup.py

Testpackages/testpackages/__init__.py

Testpackages/testpackages/mod1.py

Testpackages/testpackages/mod2.py

The sub-directory Testpackages/testpackages has the file __init__.py. This Python package is the one to install.

We'll explain the configuration of the files above so that you can package them as one distribution file and obtain the package in them as a package by Distutils.

MANIFEST.in file lists files that we will incorporate in our distribution. The contents of MANIFEST.in file is:

include README MANIFEST MANIFEST.in

include setup.py

include testpackages/*.py

The setup.py file narrates to Distutils how to package and installation distribution files. The contents of setup.py are:

#!/usr/bin/env Python

from distutils.core import setup   # [1]

long_description = 'Tests for installing and sharing

Python packages'

```
setup(name = 'testpackages',                 # [2]

    version = '1.0a',

    description = 'Tests for Python packages',

    maintainer = 'Dave katy',

    maintainer_email = 'dkaty@rexx.com',

    URL = 'http://www.rexx.com/~dkaty',

    long_description = long_description,

    packages = ['testpackages']              # [3]
    )
```

Explanation:

1. First, we import important elements from Distutils.

2. We narrate the package and its maintainer.

3. We indicate the index that will install as a package. When the distribution is installed by the user, the index and every module it contains will install as a package.

To build a distribution file, run the below code:

Python setup.py sdist --formats=gztar

It creates a file testpackages-1.0a.tar.gz under the index dist.

Then, install this distribution file by performing the following:

$ tar xvzf testpackages-1.0a.tar.gz

$ cd testpackages-1.0a

$ Python setup.py build

$ Python setup.py install   # as root

Chapter 4: Introduction to C, C++, C#

C is a programming language developed at AT&T's Bell Laboratories of the United States of America in 1972. Dennis Ritchie wrote the language. C came into existence for a particular reason, which was to design the UNIX operating system. A lot of computers utilize this system. C++ is a language developed by Bjarne Stroustrup to become a C programming language extension. The language has grown severely with time, and now contains generic, object-oriented, and functional attributes as well as provisions for low-level memory control. It executes as a compiled language, and a lot of vendors offer C++ compilers, together with the Free Software Foundation, Microsoft, etc. C++ is also very useful in software substructure applications as well as desktop applications, servers, etc. The initial developers of C# programming languages are Eric Gunnerson, Peter Golde, Peter Sollichy, Anders Hejlsberg, and Scott Wiltamuth. The architect of the C# language is Anders Hejlsberg, a lead developer at Microsoft in 2000. C# came into existence as an object-oriented programming language.

Data Types and Sizes

Regular data types in programming languages are called primitive types such as integers, characters, floating-point numbers, and so on. In C, C++, and C#. you should declare every variable before you use them, generally at the start of the function before statement execution.

C

C programming consists of four necessary date types.

- int ---- "an integer, generally displays the sizes of the integer on the host machine."

- float --- "single-precision floating-point."

- double --- "double-precision floating-point."

- char --- "a single byte, can hold a single character in the local character set."

C programming consists of five types of Specifiers. They are:

- long

- long long

- short

- unsigned

- signed

You cannot abbreviate or utilize the C language reserved keywords. The C language reserved keywords are: auto, else, long, switch, break, enum, register, typedef, case, extern, return, union, char, float, short, unsigned, const, for, signed, void, continue, goto, sizeof, volatile, default, if, static, while, do, int, struct, _Packed, double.

In C, all data types, like an integer, character, or floating-point number, contain a series of related values. Determine the value by the storage size assigned to store a specific data type within the computer memory. Storage sizes depend on your type of device. This attribute is termed "machine-dependent." For instance, an integer can occupy 32 bits on your device, or you could save it in 64 bits on another device.

C++

The C++ basic data types are identical to C. C++ also has one more type called Boolean. A Boolean can contain any of the true or false values. Express logical operations result with the use of Boolean.

C and C++ together contain 32 keywords. They are auto, else, long, switch, break, enum, register, typedef, case, extern, return, union, char, float, short, unsigned, const, for, signed, void, continue, goto, sizeof, volatile, default, if, static, while, do, int, struct, and double.

C++ does not use the keyword _Packed anymore.

C++ utilizes 30 keywords that C does not.

New keywords in C++:

Asm, dynamic cast, namespace, reinterpret_cast, bool, explicit, new, static_cast, catch, false, operator, template, class, friend, private, this, const_cast, inline, public, throw, delete, mutable, protected, true, try, typeid, typename, using, virtual, wchar_t.

C#

The C# Boolean type has a slight difference with C++. In C#, assign only two values to the Boolean type, which is true or false. While in C++, you can also assign 0 as the value to the Boolean type, which means false, and the rest means true.

Another difference between C# and C++ is integral Types. In C and C++, there is only one type for the integral type. While in C#, an integral is a group of types like the char type, it is signed or unsigned.

C# contains much more keywords than C and C++. It includes a total of 87 reserved words. All the keywords in C# are:

Abstract, as, base, bool, break by 2, byte, case, catch, char, checked, class, const, continue, decimal, default, delegate, do, double, descending 2, explicit, event, extern, else, enum, false, finally, fixed, float, for, foreach, from 2, goto, group 2, if implicit, in, int, interface, internal, into 2, is, lock, long, new, null, namespace, object, operator, out, override, orderby 2, params, private, protected, public, read-only, ref, return, switch, struct, sbyte, sealed, short, sizeof, stackalloc, static, string, select 2, this, throw, true, try, typeof, uint, ulong, unchecked, unsafe, ushort, using, var 2, virtual, volatile, void, while, where 2, yield 1.

String type

The c programming language has no string type. Therefore, the char type of array replaces it. C++ programming language contains strings of two types,

C-style and C++-style strings. A C-style string includes an array of characters stopped by the null character '\0', and its properties are above a regular array of characters. It also consists of a collection of functions to handle strings. A 'class' data type, that is how to define C++ style string. The C++ style string objects are examples of the C++ 'string' class. There is a collection of C++ string functions too.

Structure

There are two differences in the structure of C and C++ language.

1. C Structure consists of data items only, and C++ structure can include functions and data.

2. Utilizing the 'struct' keyword in the C language is required to build a variable. While in C++, you need the structure name only to locate a variable.

There is a significant difference in the structures of C++ and C#. In C++, a struct is similar to a class, only if the default access and inheritance are public instead of being private. While in C#, structs are different right from classes. C# Structs are developed to summarize insubstantial objects. Structs are value types. Therefore, they pass by value. Structs have restrictions which cannot attach to classes. For instance, they cannot be obtained from or contain base class except System.ValueType which it got from Object. Structs also do not proclaim a parameterless constructor, but they are appropriate for utilizing a class containing a little sample and are very productive, more than classes, which makes them very good for insubstantial objects development.

Inherence

Inherence means developing a new class obtained from the running class. The derived class gets every method and variables from the base class. Predominant properties and methods can enlarge the operations of a base class. C programming language does not recognize inheritance as the language is not object-oriented. C# or Java do not allow several inheritances, which means one class can inherit only one class. C++ aids various classes of inheritance. In C++, classes and structs are very similar. Structs in C# do not aid inheritance and don't assist direct default constructors while C++ structs aid various inheritances.

Array

Every subarray with several dimensional arrays should consist of similar dimensions in C and C++. In C#, arrays don't need to be equal as building jagged arrays as a single-dimensional array of arrays. The array contents are arrays that could accommodate examples of references or type to the rest of the arrays. Jagged and multidimensional arrays are quite different in C#. Multidimensional arrays in C and C++ are similar, which adjoins block with members of the same type.

Reference and Value Types

The basic types of primitive data types like short, byte, long, int, double, float, char, Boolean. Reference types are creatable classes and arrays like Scanner, String, Die, Random, String[], int[], etc. Value and reference types are quite different in C#. Primitive and reference types are the same with Simple types like long, int, double, etc. While the value type in C# are structs.

Pointer

A variable that has another variable address is a pointer. In C and C++, you can use it as Strings, arrays, codable function parameters. While in C# pointer can be proclaimed to accommodate array and value types memory address.

Partial classes

C# permit class definition to be divided over various source files though the partial classes attribute. Mark every part with the partial keyword. C and C++ do not possess this function. In C++, utilize inheritance to attain the same goal.

Chapter 5: What Is HTML?

Hypertext Markup Language (HTML) is the universal language for a one or several page project or documents developed to appear on a browser. Other languages support the HTML language such as JavaScript and Cascading Style Sheets (CSS). The browsers obtain HTML documents through the local storage or web server and then turn the file or document to multimedia pages. The structure of a page is defined by HTML in an informative manner and attach indications for the file presentation. HTML contains several elements, which are the development blocks of the language pages. HTML permits the insertion of different objects like tables, images, videos, and so on. The language also consists of different structural text semantics like paragraphs, headings, links, list, etc. HTML files are text files. Therefore, you can utilize various programs to build them like Sublime Text, Notepad++, Aptana, etc.

Anatomy of an HTML tag

Every tag in HTML programming language contains an opening and closing tag, and few contents between the tags as well as other elective attributes. Tags behave in a container manner. They give hints about data between the opening tags and closing tags.

```
<tagname atr1="val1"
atr2="val2">contents</tagname>
```

```
<tagname atr1="val1" atr2="val2">
```

Attribute

Attributes produce more information about elements contents. They are regularly placed on an element opening tag and consists of two parts: a name then a value, differentiated with an equal sign.

Basic structure of HTML

```
<!DOCTYPE html>
```

```
<html lang="en">
```

```
<head>
```

```html
<meta charset="utf-8" />

<title>Page Title</title>

</head>

<body>

</body>

</html>
```

Doctype and HTML tag

The doctype is not a tag in particular, but it should be at the beginning of all HTML page to instruct the browser on what HTML version you're using. The <!DOCTYPE> is not a case sensitive declaration. The language attribute is often attached to the opening HTML tag. The attribute is utilized to indicate an element or page language. This assists Google to interpret your page languages.

Code:

```html
<!DOCTYPE html>

<html lang="en">

</html> Head
```

The head carries the "meta" data regarding the page, data the browser needs commences operation. This head carries data regarding the page and not the data displayed within the major section of the browser window. A <title> element is always within the <head> element.

Meta tag

The meta tag is utilized to produce a page's data, and the data may be a short page description, page author, page keywords, etc. There are lots of meta tags.

Code:

```
<meta charset="utf-8" />
```

The above meta is utilized to determine your web page character encoding. We have several types of character encoding, and Unicode character encoding is the general choice for character encoding. Unicode has characters for several languages and assists on a lot of operating systems. Unicode shows various languages inside a page.

Title tag

The <title> element content displays in the browser

top, in the URL section of the page, or on that page tab.

Code:

<title>page Title</title>

Create an HTML file

1. Launch the text editor, proceed to file, and select new or tap CTRL + N.

2. Go to the Save As box on the pop up and insert your file name accompanied with the file extension .html.

3. If there is more than a single word, differentiate them with the hyphen "--," do not utilize space.

Adding text to your web page

Text is attached to a web page utilizing the following:

Paragraph

Utilize the <p> tag to develop a paragraph within HTML, to build a paragraph, place your contents within the paragraph tag, which are the opening and closing tag. The browser displays every paragraph on a new line, adding few spaces to it.

HTML

<body>

<p>

A paragraph contains a single or more sentences that create an individual unit of dialogue. The beginning of a paragraph is signified by a new line

</p>

<p>

Texts are easily understood when they are divided into bits of text. For instance, a book could contain several chapters. Chapters may contain subheadings where you can attach one or more paragraphs.

</p>

</body>

Headings

HTML programming language contains six "levels" of headings.

Utilize <h1> for main headings, utilize <h2> for subheadings and when there are additional sections within the subheadings, utilize the <h3> element, and so on. Web browsers show contents of headings in various sizes. The <h1> element contents are the biggest, and the smallest is the <h6> element. Sizes the headings are displayed by the browser can vary. Below is an example:

HTML

<body>

<h1> Main Heading</h1>

<h2> Level 2 Heading</h2>

<h3> Level 3 Heading</h3>

<h4> Level 4 Heading</h4>

<h5> Level 5 Heading</h5>

<h6> Level 5 Heading</h6>

</body>

HTML

<h1>Welcome to this outstanding website, how can

we help you?</h1>

<h2>Define html</h2>

<p>

Lorem ad minim veniam, quis nostrud exercitation ipsum dolor sit amet, consectetur adipiscing elit, sed do eiusmod dolore eu fugiat nulla. Ut enimullamco commodo reprehenderit consequat. Duis aute irure dolor in in voluptate velit laboris nisi ut aliquip ex ea esse cillum tempor incididunt ut pariaturlabore et dolore magna aliqua. </p>

<h3>Different types of HTML tags</h3>

<p>

Lorem ad minim veniam, quis nostrud exercitation ipsum dolor sit amet, consectetur adipiscing elit, sed do eiusmod dolore eu fugiat nulla. Ut enimullamco commodo reprehenderit consequat. Duis aute irure dolor in in voluptate velit laboris nisi ut aliquip ex ea esse cillum tempor incididunt ut pariaturlabore et dolore magna aliqua</p>

<h2>Define CSS</h2>

<p>

Lorem ad minim veniam, quis nostrud exercitation ipsum dolor sit amet, consectetur adipiscing elit, sed do eiusmod dolore eu fugiat nulla. Ut enimullamco commodo reprehenderit consequat. Duis aute irure dolor in in voluptate velit laboris nisi ut aliquip ex ea esse cillum tempor incididunt ut pariaturlabore et dolore magna aliqua</p>

<h3>Determine CSS selectors</h3>

<p>

Lorem ad minim veniam, quis nostrud exercitation ipsum dolor sit amet, consectetur adipiscing elit, sed do eiusmod dolore eu fugiat nulla. Ut enimullamco commodo reprehenderit consequat. Duis aute irure dolor in in voluptate velit laboris nisi ut aliquip ex ea esse cillum tempor incididunt ut pariaturlabore et dolore magna aliqua</p>

White space

If there are a lot of spaces on the text editor the web browser handles it as one space. When it finds a line break, it handles it as one-line space. You can call this process white space collapsing.

HTML

```html
<body>

<h1>White space</h1>

<h2>Without white space</h2>

<p>The browser ignores white like this</p>

<h2>With spaces</h2>

<p>The browser will display this       white space

</p>

<h2>Browser ignores line spaces</h2>

<p>The browser will disregard this line spaces

</p>

</body>
```

Line Breaks

Utilize this tag <br> to build a line break while using HTML.

HTML

```html
<body>
```

<p>The world
gets two thousand tons every day
 because of the space dust.

</p>

</body>

Horizontal Rule

Utilize the <h> to build a long horizontal line

HTML

<p>

Lorem ad minim veniam, quis nostrud exercitation ipsum dolor sit amet, consectetur adipiscing elit, sed do eiusmod dolore eu fugiat nulla. Ut enimullamco commodo reprehenderit consequat. Duis aute irure dolor in in voluptate velit laboris nisi ut aliquip ex ea esse cillum tempor incididunt ut pariaturlabore et dolore magna aliqua </p>

<p>

Lorem ad minim veniam, quis nostrud exercitation ipsum dolor sit amet, consectetur adipiscing elit, sed do eiusmod dolore eu fugiat nulla. Ut enimullamco commodo reprehenderit consequat. Duis aute irure dolor in in voluptate velit laboris nisi ut aliquip ex ea esse cillum tempor incididunt ut pariaturlabore et dolore magna aliqua</p>

<p>

Lorem ad minim veniam, quis nostrud exercitation ipsum dolor sit amet, consectetur adipiscing elit, sed do eiusmod dolore eu fugiat nulla. Ut enimullamco commodo reprehenderit consequat. Duis aute irure dolor in in voluptate velit laboris nisi ut aliquip ex ea esse cillum tempor incididunt ut pariaturlabore et dolore magna aliqua</p>

<hr>

<p>

Lorem ad minim veniam, quis nostrud exercitation ipsum dolor sit amet, consectetur adipiscing elit, sed do eiusmod dolore eu fugiat nulla. Ut enimullamco commodo reprehenderit consequat. Duis aute irure dolor in in voluptate velit laboris nisi ut aliquip ex ea esse cillum tempor incididunt ut pariaturlabore et dolore magna aliqua </p>

<p>

Lorem ad minim veniam, quis nostrud exercitation ipsum dolor sit amet, consectetur adipiscing elit, sed do eiusmod dolore eu fugiat nulla. Ut enimullamco commodo reprehenderit consequat. Duis aute irure dolor in in voluptate velit laboris nisi ut aliquip ex ea esse cillum tempor incididunt ut pariaturlabore et dolore magna aliqua</p>

<p>

Lorem ad minim veniam, quis nostrud exercitation ipsum dolor sit amet, consectetur adipiscing elit, sed do eiusmod dolore eu fugiat nulla. Ut enimullamco commodo reprehenderit consequat. Duis aute irure dolor in in voluptate velit laboris nisi ut aliquip ex ea esse cillum tempor incididunt ut pariaturlabore et dolore magna aliqua</p>

Strong tag

The <strong> element signifies content of solid significance. For instance, the content within this element could be used with strong emphasis. Browsers displays the texts of a <strong> element in bold format. This attribute primary use is to bolden texts.

HTML

<p>

<strong>Beware:</strong> Beware of women this area.

</p>

<p>

I'm thinking of heading to Germany <strong> but I cannot find my passport.

</strong>

</p>

Quotations

You can utilize these two elements for quotations marking: The <q> element and <blockquote>.

<blockquote>

The <blockquote> element is utilized for larger quotes which takes a whole paragraph. Browsers would align the <blockquote> element text. Do not utilize this element to align just contents instead utilize CSS.

HTML

`<p>`

Lorem ad minim veniam, quis nostrud exercitation Ipsum dolor sit amet, consectetur adipiscing elit, sed do eiusmod dolore eu fugiat nulla. Ut enimullamco commodo reprehenderit consequat. Duis aute irure dolor in voluptate velit laboris nisi ut aliquip ex ea esse cillum tempor incididunt ut pariaturlabore et dolore Magna aliqua`</p>`

`<blockquote cite="http:/www.google.com/ ">`

`<p>`

Lorem ad minim veniam, quis nostrud exercitation Ipsum dolor sit amet, consectetur adipiscing elit, sed do eiusmod dolore eu fugiat nulla. Ut enimullamco commodo reprehenderit consequat. Duis aute irure dolor in voluptate velit laboris nisi ut aliquip ex ea esse cillum tempor incididunt ut pariaturlabore et dolore Magna aliqua`</p>`

`</blockquote>`

`<p>`

Lorem ad minim veniam, quis nostrud exercitation

Ipsum dolor sit amet, consectetur adipiscing elit, sed do eiusmod dolore eu fugiat nulla. Ut enimullamco commodo reprehenderit consequat. Duis aute irure dolor in voluptate velit laboris nisi ut aliquip ex ea esse cillum tempor incididunt ut pariaturlabore et dolore Magna aliqua.

</p>

<q>

Utilize the <q> element for smaller quotes that are inside a paragraph. Browsers should place quotes across the <q> element, but Internet Explorer doesn't. So, programmers avoid the <q> element. Its value contains a URL that holds additional information regarding the quotation source.

HTML

<body>

Lorem ipsum dolor sits amet, consectetur adipisicing elit, <q>do eiusmod tempor incididunt ut labore et dolore Magna aliqua</q> Ut enim ad minim veniam,quis nos exercitation ullamco laboris nisi ut aliquip ex ea commodoconsequat.

```
</body>
```

Abbreviation

Utilize the <abbr> element to build abbreviations. The opening tag containing a title attribute is utilized to indicate the full meaning.

HTML

```
<abbr title="International monetary funds">I.M.F</abbr>
```

Superscript

The <sup> element is utilized to hold superscript characters like the dates suffixes or mathematical methods such as raising a number to a power of 2.

HTML

```
<p>25<sup>th</sup> of October is my birthday</p>
```

Chapter 6: HTML Lists

There are several reasons to attach a list into your pages. You can create three types of lists in HTML, they are:

Ordered list

Unordered list

Definition list

Ordered list

The HTML <ol> element stands for an ordered list of things, which outputs it in a numbered manner. In an ordered list, you can utilize any of these numbers (1, 2, 3), and alphabets (A, B, C), as well as Roman numerals (i, ii, iii) to set the items on the list.

HTML

<h2>Countries in the world</h2>

<ol>

<li>Australia</li>

<li>Germany</li>

```html
<li>Brazil</li>
```

```html
<li>United states of America</li>
```

```html
</ol>
```

Unordered list

An unordered list is a group of identical items that contain no unique order or succession. The list is built through the use of the HTML <ul> tag. Every list item list is indicated with a bullet. To create a bullet-point list, write the list inside the <ul> element (that means unordered list). Your bullet points should be enclosed within opening <li> and closing </li> tags ("li" means list item).

HTML

```html
<h2> Countries in the world </h2>
```

```html
<ul>
```

```html
<li>France</li>
```

```html
<li>Bolivia</li>
```

```html
<li>Peru</li>
```

```html
<li>Azerbaijan</li>
```

```html
</ul>
```

Description list

The description list is a unique type of list for terms accompanied by a small text definition or text description. Description lists are enclosed within the <dl> element. The <dl> element also has a <dt> and <dd> description elements within. You will define the <dt> element content. The <dd> element holds the previous <dt> element description.

HTML

<dl>

<dt>Define HTML</dt>

<dd>

Lorem ad minim veniam, quis nostrud exercitation Ipsum dolor sit amet, consectetur adipiscing elit, sed do eiusmod dolore eu fugiat nulla. Ut enimullamco commodo reprehenderit consequat. Duis aute irure dolor in voluptate velit laboris nisi ut aliquip ex ea esse cillum tempor incididunt ut pariaturlabore et dolore Magna aliqua

</dd>

<dt>Define CSS</dt>

<dd>

Lorem ad minim veniam, quis nostrud exercitation Ipsum dolor sit amet, consectetur adipiscing elit, sed do eiusmod dolore eu fugiat nulla. Ut enimullamco commodo reprehenderit consequat. Duis aute irure dolor in voluptate velit laboris nisi ut aliquip ex ea esse cillum tempor incididunt ut pariaturlabore et dolore Magna aliqua

</dd>

<dt>Define Javascript</dt>

<dd>

Lorem ad minim veniam, quis nostrud exercitation Ipsum dolor sit amet, consectetur adipiscing elit, sed do eiusmod dolore eu fugiat nulla. Ut enimullamco commodo reprehenderit consequat. Duis aute irure dolor in voluptate velit laboris nisi ut aliquip ex ea esse cillum tempor incididunt ut pariaturlabore et dolore Magna aliqua

</dd>

</dl>

Nested list

The nested list means a list created inside another list.

You can include a sub-list within the <li> element. Web browsers output nested lists in an organized manner a little bit away from the parent list. In a nested unordered list, the browser transforms the list style to bullet point.

HTML

<h2>Countries in the world</h2>

<ul>

 <li>United states of America</li>

 <li>Germany

<ul>

 <li>Spain</li>

 <li>Canada</li>

 <li>Hungary</li>

 <li>Brazil</li>

</ul>

</li>

 <li>Sweden</li>

 <li>France</li>

</ul>

Links

The defining attribute of the web is the link because links enable users to migrate from a web page to another. You can create a list utilizing the <a> element. Contents within the opening <a> and closing </a> can be clicked. You indicate the page you're linking to utilizing the href attribute.

Linking to another site

The anchor tag is used to link in HTML code, the <a> tag. Follow the "a" within the tag with an attribute. If you want to link to other web pages, accompany the "a" with an "href." If you want to link to a separate website, the href attribute value should be the website full web address, you can call that an absolute URL.

By default, Links are shown in blue with an underline by web browsers.

HTML

<a href="http://google.com">Google</a>

Links that open a new tab

Utilize the opening <a> tag target attribute to enable a link open in a new window. _blank should be the attribute value.

HTML

```
<a href="http://google.com"
target="_blank">Google</a>
```

Link to other pages on the same site

The opening <a> tag must carry the href attribute. The href attribute value would be the linked file's name.

HTML

```
<a href="index.html">Home</a>
```

Linking to a specific part of the same page

In cases of a long web page, and you want to link to a particular section of that page to avoid scrolling up and down the page to locate that section. The destination anchor permits the author to indicate particular points within a page that a source anchor point. Example of linking to a particular page section on web pages include:

"Back to top" – this is often under a long page.

HTML

```
<body>

<h2>Linking and Navigation</h2>

    <p>This        page      explains      the       following
languages</p>

<ul>

    <li><a href="#html">Define Html</a></li>

    <li><a href="#CSS">Define CSS</a></li>

    <li><a                   href="#JavaScript">Define
JavaScript</a></li>

</ul>

<h3 id="html">Define Html</h3>

    <p>Lorem  ad  minim  veniam,  quis  nostrud
```

exercitation Ipsum dolor sit amet, consectetur adipiscing elit, sed do eiusmod dolore eu fugiat nulla. Ut enimullamco commodo reprehenderit consequat. Duis aute irure dolor in voluptate velit laboris nisi ut aliquip ex ea esse cillum tempor incididunt ut pariaturlabore et dolore Magna aliqua </p>

<a href="#top">back to top</a>

<h3 id="CSS">Define CSS</h3>

<p>Lorem ad minim veniam, quis nostrud exercitation Ipsum dolor sit amet, consectetur adipiscing elit, sed do eiusmod dolore eu fugiat nulla. Ut enimullamco commodo reprehenderit consequat. Duis aute irure dolor in voluptate velit laboris nisi ut aliquip ex ea esse cillum tempor incididunt ut pariaturlabore et dolore Magna aliqua </p>

<a href="#top">back to top</a>

<h3 id="JavaScript">Define JavaScript</h3>

<p>Lorem ad minim veniam, quis nostrud exercitation Ipsum dolor sit amet, consectetur adipiscing elit, sed do eiusmod dolore eu fugiat nulla. Ut enimullamco commodo reprehenderit consequat. Duis aute irure dolor in voluptate velit laboris nisi ut aliquip ex ea esse cillum tempor incididunt ut pariaturlabore et dolore Magna aliqua </p>

<a href="#top">back to top</a>

</body>

Link to a particular part of another page

Linking to a particular section of a separate page is easy to accomplish. Make sure the page you are linking to contains id attributes that specify the particular section of the page. You can attach the syntax to the end of that page link. So, the href attribute will hold the page address (absolute or relative URL), accompanied by the # syntax, and then utilize the id attribute value on the linking element. For instance, the code is written like this: <a href="http:/www.htmlandcssbook.com#bottom">\

Links to other files (ZIP files, Word documents, PDFs, etc.)

Place a link on items such as images and pdf drives and not just text. If you want to share PDF file with others, write the code would like this:

HTML

<a href="html.docx">Download my CV</a>

Chapter 7: What is Coding

Just as the saying goes, coding runs the world. Although a whole lot of people do not realize it exists or what it even means. The first act of writing in a programming language is called coding. Let me take you through a little process. Launch your web browser and right click on any part of your browser window, and click View Page Source. Now ask yourself, do you understand what you see? They are written codes mostly written in HTML programming language with bits of CSS and JavaScript. Coding is a script that the computer understands. The script can command the computer to do your bidding if your code right.

Your computer does not understand your chain of codes at all. The machine only understands Yes and No or Binary codes (1 and 0). The programming language that you write only tells the computer what to do. The computer speaks Binary, but understands several programming languages just like you know programming and your native language.

Why You Should Learn Coding

Coding can have a massive influence on your professional and life. Below are a few reasons why you should learn and understand coding.

Coding hugely increases your potential earnings. Professional programmers and coders charge high hourly rates. A lot of professional coders will reject hourly rate short of $100 per hour, which is a fantastic income. The best part of it is that there is a scarcity of coders, which means extra profit.

Coding lets you work for yourself. Although there are lots of coders working on more significant contract's at large companies all around the world, you can also work in freelance roles. Being a freelance coder, and it gives you the capacity to choose where to work and when and how you want to.

You work on your projects. Being a coder gives you the ability to develop websites and you're really only limited by your imagination.

Types of Coders

You need to understand that there are several types of

coders, and each one focuses on separate things. Coders can become game developers, systems engineers, and AI programmers, etc.

Front-End Developer

Front-end developers are website builders. They handle the layout, design, and appearance on a webpage through the use of front-end languages like CSS, JavaScript, and HTML.

A few functions of front-end web developers are writing the code layout of a design and transforming it into a website. They create functional and interactive websites. It includes things like building hyperlinked buttons, placing animations, etc.

Back-End Developer

The back-end developer develops web apps that run the website. Web apps are designed to perform a particular task.

A few functions of back-end web developers are the creation of an account on a website, logging in and out of a website, building profiles, and connecting with friends on social media.

Chapter 8: Introduction to Raspberry Pi

The Raspberry Pi is a sequence of little single-board computers built in the United Kingdom. Raspberry Pi Foundation established Raspberry Pi to enhance the knowledge of computer science basics in institutions and developed countries. The authentic Raspberry Pi model became more popular than expected. It sold above its expected target for uses like robotics without peripherals (keyboards and mice). A few accessories are available in various bundles (official and unofficial).

The Ingredients for a Raspberry Pi 2

USB ports

The Raspberry Pi 2 contains four USB ports, and it lets you attach it to mice, keyboards, USB sticks and WiFi dongles holding all of your documents. The ports do not supply a lot of power; therefore, if you would attach a USB hub to the Pi, find the one with an additional power supply.

Ethernet port

The old way to get an internet connection is through a wire named Ethernet cable. Locate these ports at the router's rear which allows you attach the Raspberry Pi to it directly. This concept is set up quickly, unlike WiFi, and supplies better internet, but it is limited by the cable length.

GPIO header

It contains the all-purpose input/output (GPIO) pins. GPIO pins are a group of connections with several functions, but their primary function lets you attach the Raspberry Pi to an electronic circuit. Then you can program the Pi to influence the circuit and perform beautiful things with it.

Audio out

It looks similar to a headphone socket, a 3.5mm jack precisely, this enables the connection of the Pi to the device speakers, or your headphones and contain a Raspberry jam.

MicroSD card slot

Utilize a small SD card as the hard drive of the Raspberry Pi. Many systems cannot be attached directly to a microSD card; therefore, you will need an adaptor that goes into the SD card slots.

Power

It is the small charging port within your smartphone. It is a micro-USB port, and it means that the Pi can be powered with the right phone charger or through the PC. It is advisable to utilize the official Raspberry Pi power supply to ensure the Pi gets the right amount of power.

HDMI port

It is the kind of port located at the back of modern televisions as well as the monitors of computers. Utilize HDMI cable to attach the Raspberry Pi to the screen to watch what it does.

Configuration Tool Tabs

There are four tabs in the Raspberry Pi Configuration. They let you develop several parts of your Pi.

System

With the system, you can fix the Pi boots to the command line (CLI), create autologin, and alter the password. It also contains an overscan setting that helps eradicate the black border across the desktop if one exists.

Interfaces

Several interfaces on the Raspberry Pi can be allowed or disallowed below this tab, which includes camera and connectors.

Performance

You can develop GPU memory allocation to enhance performance to execute a specific operation.

Localization

This tab lets you develop the right language, keyboard layout, and time zone.

Software Configuration Tool

When Raspbian has loaded and displays on the desktop, select Menu to launch the main menu. Choose the Preferences option and tool Configuration on the submenu. It creates a tool that is utilized to configure several options on the Raspberry Pi. Note that the essential choice to change is the Expand Filesystem option. Raspbian does not need a lot of space to run, so you should tell it to utilize every available space on the SD card to store files if you want it that way. So, select the Expand Filesystem on the Pi Configuration menu, and reload the Pi when prompted. Select Shutdown, and choose Reboot, then tap OK.

Set Up Your Raspberry Pi

Download NOOBS

There are lots of operating systems that comes with the Raspberry Pi that you can utilize. You can install them manually. Although there is an easy way to install the OSes, which is through the NOOBS or Out of Box Software. It contains every new version of the

Raspberry Pi operating system. Utilize NOOBS full version because it includes Raspbian already, which makes the operation slightly faster rather than NOOBS Lite.

Install SD Card

Get the SD card ready to function correctly on the Raspberry Pi. Remove every vital documents or information because you will have to format the SD card. Install the SD Card Formatter 4.0 instrument to get the card ready. Format the SD card and remove the files within the NOOBS zip folder then place them on the card. Now NOOBS prepared to be used on the SD card.

Connect the Cables

Remove the SD card adaptor, extract the microSD card, then place it in the Raspberry Pi. Plug an HDMI cable in between the screen and the Raspberry Pi, the router's Ethernet cable (or USB WIFI dongle), together with a keyboard and mouse. Then connect the power cable to Raspberry Pi.

Install Raspbian

When the Raspberry Pi turns on, it will show few

screen texts, disregard it until it reaches a menu that lists every operating system. It lets you choose several OSes at a go, but right, we will focus on Raspbian. Choose Raspbian, select Install, and the installation operation begins, which could take some time to finish execution.

Installing and Updating Software

Install New Software

When you install the Raspbian, it gives you access to a lot of several programs. Raspbian can be installed through the use of terminal because Raspbian has no app store. Utilize the below command to find the Raspbian on the terminal:

$ apt-cache search FTP

It sends back packages with details. Utilize the package name to install any of the software, but for us, FileZilla returns as FTP client. FileZilla is the package name. To install, we use:

sudo apt-get install FileZilla

The above will download the package and all required software needed to run the package, then install to Raspbian.

Update Your Software and OS

Raspbian software periodically updates online, and it fixes security updates and bugs. They do not sync automatically with Raspberry Pi; always check for updates on your system. The terminal handles this operation similar to software installation. The update process is of two parts: firstly, update repositories (list of software and versions available on your system). Achieve that by inputting the command:

sudo apt-get update

It checks online to see the software repositories state and gives result to Raspberry Pi, and it will save changes. It then decides which software to be updated, but instruct it to execute the update with the following command:

sudo apt-get upgrade

The Raspbian operating system may require a significant or massive update or significant changes like a browser or new interface, etc. It doesn't happen regularly, but when it occurs, execute the upgrade with:

sudo apt dist-upgrade

Chapter 9: Introduction to Black-Hat Hacking

The word "hacker" alone has amassed a lot of negative feelings. Traits like breaking into devices and stealing sensitive and private information are usually what you hear about hackers. A large population of the world's computer users has gone through the effects of hacking activities which includes spyware attacks, virus attacks, and various types of malware that penetrate, slow down, or damage your device. Anyway, it is not every hacker that is deceitful and untrustworthy, who offer nothing other than privacy violations. The word "hacker" has a good and useful meaning. Traditionally, a hacker is a person who enjoys attempting to improve computers and other electronics. They get to know everything about the computer system and functions and then do the work to search for ways to improve them. In other words, hackers are the people to turn to when it comes to enhancing your computers and making your device function better and faster. But in today's world, a black-hat hacker is a person that obtains electronic information without permission, by dubious gains, and for self interest. Although many ethical hackers exist, they are white-hat hackers, while the suspicious and corrupt hackers are called the black-hat hackers. To apprehend a hacker, you need another hacker to do the job and catch the hacker, and to your advantage, there are lots of ethical hackers who are willing to get the job done. Hacking is also a computer skill that you can use both ways, good or bad.

Objectives of Hacking

The world's perception today about hackers is the black-hat hacker's way, the act of obtaining vital information dubiously. Ethical hacking is utilized to discover your device or network weak points and get them secured so the black hats do not have access to transform or manipulate and use your information against you. The motive of white-hat hackers is to run security checks, fix all loopholes, and ensure information and device security. The white hat section has adopted a different name, and they call themselves penetration testing specialists. One rule that helps you to differentiate between penetration testing and dubious hackers is that the white-hat hackers get the permission of device owners before they breach their security. During that operation, when the penetration testing completes, the device owner receives a very secure network or device system. When the entire penetration testing process ends, the hacker then recommends few security solutions and how to fix problems.

The Caveat

One thing you cannot expect is to have everything protected. The idea of totally securing any device, computer, or electronic system from potential attacks is farfetched. You can achieve that only by unplugging the device from all possible networks and keeping it safe far from all contacts. That renders the contained information useless to everyone. In the hacking world, it is tough to plan for anything because there are a lot of unknowns in this incredibly connected game. You should also know that the next time you turn on your WiFi and allow your friends to connect, you have just created a way for hackers to get in. Let's talk about some general security liabilities black-hat hackers relate with and monitor closely.

Network Infrastructure Attacks

Network infrastructure attacks can bypass and get into local networks and on the Internet. Too many systems are accessible through the internet, which makes it very easy to break. You can hack into a system by attaching a modem to the local network. Another concept of a network intrusion is through NetBIOS, TCP/IP, and several transport mechanisms inside a network. Other tricks are building denial services by sending a massive number of requests. You can use network analyzers to get data packets that move across the web. They examine the data they get and disclose the information they contain. Another trick is when WiFi networks are not protected. You must have heard too many stories of people moving around with tablets, laptops, or smartphones searching for unprotected WiFi signal to manipulate.

Non-Technical Attacks

This type of attack involves tricking people into disclosing their passwords, willingly or not. It is similar to social engineering, and that is the exact tool utilized for these types of attacks. One example is paying, duping, or bribing a colleague to disclose usernames and passwords. Another concept of non-technical hack is other people's computer room, load the system, and then extract every piece of needed information. Yes, it sounds like the most comfortable thing on earth. In reality, non-technical hacks are an integral part of the hacking tactics.

Attacks on an Operating System

The operating system attacks are regularly performed hacks. There are a lot of computers out there without any protection. Therefore, there are various loopholes in a lot of operating systems. Even the newest ones contain a few bugs that hackers can manipulate. One of the ways to hack the operating system is through hacking the password or attacking the encryption mechanisms.

Attacks on Applications

Online applications that use internet connectivity get thousands of attacks (web applications and email server software applications). One attack type is spam mail, which goes back as far as the year 2000. Spam mail contains a lot of things that can break into your device. You can also utilize malware or harmful software to attack a lot of things, and the primary target is apps. Software programs like worms, trojan horses, spyware, and viruses. These programs can access your device online. Another type of applications attacked regularly is Simple Mail Transfer Protocols applications (SMTP) and Hypertext Transfer Protocols applications (HTTP). A lot of these apps bypass firewalls of computer users automatically. You should know all these tricks to provide excellent protection to your computer system from a powerful attack.

Hacking Basics

This section explains some essential hacking tools and techniques. These tools are available in several hacking methods. These are the most straightforward form of black-hat hacking you can learn.

Social Engineering

A non-technical hack is called social engineering. It means using the regularly used available resources to users and companies. When it comes to companies, the company's employees are the target. People put their trust in other people by nature. It is a loophole for hackers to manipulate any organization. They only need to get the details from one person, and then they can utilize those details to obtain additional information from another coworker, and the trend continues. For example, a computer hacker could pose as a computer repair or tech support rep and approach a particular company. They often tell companies employees to download a few free software or subscribe to a service that they can manipulate easily. Sometimes a black-hat hacker boldly asks for the company username and password. Phishing sites also offer the same services. These websites are created to collate information. Some sites contain several similar visual layouts or patterns like the original site. They trick customers of a particular website into signing into a lookalike website. These websites then collate the customers' passwords and usernames. Black-hat hackers can obtain PayPal logins, credit card information, and several important pieces of information. With social engineering concept of hacking, you only need to look official and professional to a total stranger.

Social Engineering Basic Steps

The first thing to do is to collate data about a particular company or personnel. Hackers perform these research themselves. Then, they utilize the information with finance organizations, the SEC, and every bit of valuable information. The larger the company, the more you can obtain information about it. Hackers find their way into the company's trash to get information. A lot of employees dump a lot of enticing documents such as printed emails, meeting notes, network diagrams, organizational charts, and several lists of employee's phone numbers into the trash can. The black-hat hackers build trust. They contact customers or employees utilizing obtained information. They pretend to be one of the company's personnel and acts nicely and ready to be of help. Hackers communicate victims through chat, emails, or voicemail to look official and professional.

Countermeasures to Social Engineering

The best way to counter social engineering concept of hacking is to ensure you notify the public. Ensure your employees and customers are up to date of your official communication protocol and to be cautious of anybody who demands login information or any valuable information.

Compromising Physical Security Flaws

One significant part of information security is the physical security. Physical security hackers can bypass and break into their computers. They cannot avoid the company's firewall but can attach a hardware or software component in your network within your firewall by coming into your computer room and attach a tool into one employee's device. Some hackers want more than connecting a tool and bypass your security from within, and some would access and steal vital information. They can sneak into your organization through the employee smoking areas, cafeteria doors, or any available entry point.

Hacking Passwords

Password hacking is one of the hackers' favorites. It can be achieved using social engineering and endangering physical liabilities within the workplace. One way to hack another person's password is to spy on them when they input it on a device. Password hacking is one usual way for hackers to obtain data through a computer network. Another method, called inference, enables hackers to collate as much data of an employee such as birthdates, children names, favorite things, phone numbers, favorite TV shows, and others. Hackers use these when trying to guess your password. There are several top-notch tech ways to guess other people's password. The tools to hack a password include a few remote cracking services, network analyzers, and several types of software to crack a password. You probably must have heard about application programs using brute force. It is a trial-and-error concept of password guessing. Brute force tries every possible combination to achieve the password. It takes time before they acquire the password. It is a crucial exhaustive search concept.

Many hackers focus on physical flaws and break into people's computer to find their passwords. Microsoft operating systems often save passwords within the same directory called the security accounts manager (SAM). Sometimes the operating system saves passwords inside an existing database file, such as ntds.dit as an example. Users develop emergency repair disks within a USB drive. What you need to do is access the directory (for example, c:\winnt\repair). You can find passwords within the system's registry. Some employees also store passwords in text files, which is easy for hackers to obtain. Another method is to install keyloggers. They can be bits of software or hardware which logs the keystrokes of unaware users. There are a lot of keystroke logging software programs that you can buy, and some are even free.

Network Hacking

Hacking a network is an operation of too many forms. One instance is when people break into other people's internet or WiFi connection to browse for free. Within a network, make sure you scan the network to search for unprotected connected network device connected. Now access the data. One instance for that is the moment you are logged to a WiFi network, launch your windows explorer and select Network. Then check the file sharing and network discovery. If it is within that specific network, search for a connected device to access the documents within it.

War Dialing

If you intend to understand the old ways of breaking into other people's network, then war dialing is your target and will fulfill your desires. This concept of hacking utilizes the advantage of liabilities in other people's telephone system. The idea requires the use of war dialing software. Hackers can identify repeat dial tones and password inputs at the dial tone and place calls to any locations freely. Hackers can access voicemail for phone systems utilizing PBX switches.

Network Structure Vulnerabilities

You can find vulnerabilities on every computer network. No matter how small the weaknesses are, hackers can always exploit it. The utensils required for network hacking is the same tools necessary to identify defects within your network. Devices such as network scanners, DNS lookups, and require network queries.

Few scanners can perform ping sweeps and port scanning. Other scanners can also perform SMTP relay testing. You require a scanner that performs host port probing and operating system fingerprinting as well as testing firewalls. Port scanners can list the devices on your network. Port scanners are easy to utilize, and you can test any device with one. Every regular hacked port utilizes the TCP protocols but while some utilize UDP. The regular ports and services related to them are 23 (Telnet), 22 (SSH), 7 (Echo), 53 (DNS), 21 (FTP control), 80 (HTTP), 25 (SMTP), 443 (HTTPS), 19 (Chargen), 1433 (Microsoft SQL Server), and 20 (FTP data) and so on.

Breaking into WiFi Networks

Wireless networks used at home, cafes, offices, or anywhere are all vulnerable to hacking. Gone are those days that open WiFi networks are secured. It means that you can hack any connected device to the internet through wireless. Hackers only need to find free public networks. Anybody can get online and break into your internet. The only safeguard measure for people against hackers is the signal range from the WiFi router. Those were the days of signal amplifiers and antennas. The only available security to WiFi router users was Wireless Encryption Protocol (WEP). Although with this, hackers can monitor you and will crack your WEP code because the design is poor. Nowadays, there is no need for WiFi signal limits. A lot of routers consist of 1,500 feet range, about 500 meters. The only difference from the old ways is that new routers utilize WiFi Protected Access (WPA) and WPA2 (WIFI Protected Access 2) to be their security protocols type, and they are better than WEP. To hack into your friend's WiFi connection, make sure you monitor the WiFi activity and grab the data when they log their device onto the access point or router. It looks like a difficult task, but there is a way to go around it. You only need to dispatch a death frame. They are packets which you will transfer to the access point like the wireless router that disconnects all other connected devices to that particular network. They will have to log in again, then you can apprehend the login data itself.

Tools for Hacking into Wireless Connections

There are lots of wireless connections hacking tools available today. There is a payment attached to get premium quality of some while there is also some open-source (free) ones which will perform decently.

Search and download the penetration testing software (Aircrackng and so on). Wireless penetration programs can apprehend pcap (packet capture) files. Apprehending takes about one hour. Now ask yourself, what do I do with this packet capture files? Some penetration testing software evaluates the information for you. However, if you are using a free penetration testing software and functionality is limited, then another tool is needed to crack the packet capture files. These tools are called password crackers. There are few free password crackers while others come at a price. You need to install some on your device while the rest are online applications. The primary operation of the password crackers tool is to check the packet capture files against a database that contains millions of passwords. Sometimes it takes minutes or even seconds to crack passwords with these tools. Cracking software often breaks the PIN into several equal halves. The pin contains eight characters. You need to understand that the pin last character of that pin is only a checksum. It means that the first seven are only digits/characters that would crack. Make sure you do not transmit its SSID, which is the assigned name to the wireless network by the user. Few routers contain MAC filtering that permits only listed computers to gain entry the wireless network. The apprehended MAC addresses can be copied and used as your own. That process is called spoofing.

Hacking Your Own Windows Password

A lot of people have this habit of forgetting passwords, and this occurs each day. So, what happens when anyone or even you can forget your password and cannot log into your personal computer. It is one kind of situation that you are going to enjoy your hacking skills. However, it is essential to know that hacking into people's computers is illegal, and you can only do that when you are paid to do the job.

Default Administrator Account

Let's assume that you possess a machine running on Windows 7. One of the ways to achieve your goal is to utilize the default Windows 7 Administrator account. It is often disabled when you launch the device in normal mode. So, reload the machine in Safe Mode. Then choose default administrator on Windows 7. The default administrator requires no password. When you get to that stage, leave the password box blank and click log in. When you are in, you can head to the Control panel and modify the password giving you troubles.

Password Reset Disk

This disk can also be called the password reset file. It has a little wizard program which guides users to develop new passwords for Windows user account that you forgot the password. Develop this disk when you install the operating system. Attach the plug to the device and select Reset Password. Now follow the prompts. It will demand to know where it can find the reset password files, so choose the right drive. The prompt will tell you to create a new password. Now follow the prompt instructions.

Conclusion

This book carries vital information about the Python programming language, C, C++, C#, HTML, Coding, Raspberry PI, and Black Hat Hacking. The concepts this book contains will help you understand advanced Python regular expressions, Iterator Objects, Extending and embedding Python, Parsing, Creating a parser with pyparsing, GUI Applications, Guidance on Packages and Modules, Built-in Data Types and so on. As you finish this book, you have learned quite a lot about Python, C, C++, C#, HTML, Coding, Black Hat Hacking, setting up your Raspberry Pi, installing and updating software, using the GPIO pins to hacking Basics, network hacking basics, and hacking your own windows password.

References

A Python Book: Advanced Python. Retrieved from
https://www.davekuhlman.org/python_book_01.pdf

HTML5 Step by Step. Retrieved from
http://michael-
puff.de/Programmierung/HTML/Step%20by%20Ste
p%20HTML5.pdf

Coding tutorial. Retrieved from
https://www.bitdegree.org/tutorials/what-is-coding/

THE Official RASPBERRY PI. Retrieved from
https://www.raspberrypi.org/magpi-
issues/Projects_Book_v1.pdf

Computer Hacking. Retrieved from
file:///C:/Users/hp/Downloads/Computer%20Hacki
ng_%20A%20beginners%20guide%20to%20compute
r%20hacking%20%20(%20PDFDrive.com%20).pdf

Lorem Ipsum. Retrieved from
https://www.lipsum.com/